MORE
Pets with
Tourette's

**Mike Lepine &
Mark Leigh**

summersdale

MORE PETS WITH TOURETTE'S

Summersdale Publishers Ltd
46 West Street
Chichester
West Sussex
PO19 1RP
UK

www.summersdale.com

Printed and bound by Imago

ISBN: 978-1-84024-698-8

Disclaimer

No animals were harmed in the making of this book,
but some have had their social standing diminished.

Meet the authors

Mike Lepine thinks this is his most intellectual book to date, in that it is a Dadaist response to liberal suppression of dissenting voices. Honest. Being an artistic statement (and incidentally far funnier than anything by Damien Hirst) you can proudly and confidently display *More Pets with Tourette's* on your coffee table or make it the topic of choice at your next dinner party.

Mark Leigh hopes this book raises awareness of this cruel and terrible affliction that affects so many innocent pets. This invidious condition wrecks lives, puts an immense strain on relationships with owners and can lead to very embarrassing moments at Crufts, as well as a lifetime ban. Mark lives in Surrey with his family and owns a Cavalier King Charles spaniel called Lulabelle who likes to say 'ringpiece'.

PETS WITH TOURETTE'S

Mike Lepine & Mark Leigh

£5.99   **Hardback**   **ISBN: 978 1 84024 610 0**

Oh dear. It seems that our furry friends have been afflicted with a bad case of the swearing tic (not the wriggly kind you remove from your dog's back).

From foul-mouthed Fidos to fish that say 'f***!', *Pets with Tourette's* combines comical and cute photos with inappropriate captions to tickle the belly of animal lovers everywhere.

'... instantly draws the eye!... provides endless amusement and will have you laughing for hours'
Borderslocal.co.uk

'guaranteed to tickle anyone's sense of humour'
SUNDAY SPORT

'Book of the year!'   **POPBITCH**

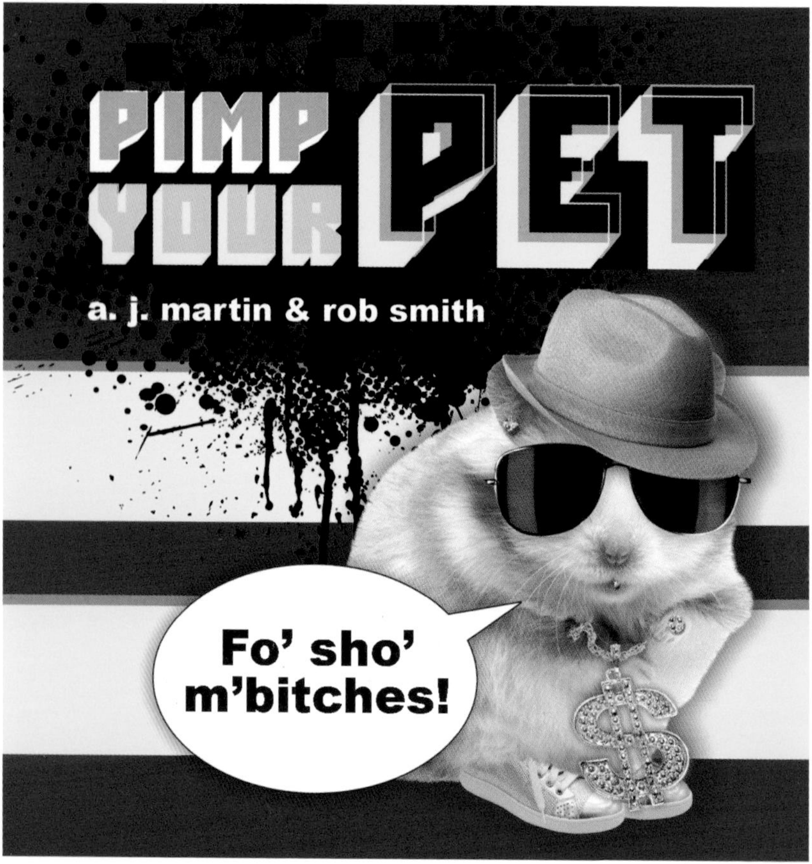
PIMP YOUR PET
a. j. martin & rob smith
Fo' sho' m'bitches!

PIMP YOUR PET

A. J. Martin & Rob Smith

£5.99   Hardback   ISBN: 978 1 84024 713 8

Does your pet have a secret yearning to be someone else for a day? When Burt the budgie is bashing ten bells out of his mirror, is he perhaps re-enacting Robert de Niro in *Taxi Driver* (You talkin' to me?).

Pimp Your Pet contains all you need to unleash your furry friend's alter-ego, including simple cut-outs with tabs and classic one-liners to help your pet get into character, with everything from gangsta' rapper get-ups to superhero kits to choose from.

www.summersdale.com